GOD SEES YOUR NOT YET

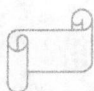

God Sees Your Not Yet

By: The Reverend Carlton R. Worthen, M.Div.

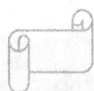

Carlton Worthen Publishing Atlanta, GA

Copyright © 2012 by Carlton Worthen

ISBN-13: 978-0692357934
(Carlton Worthen Publishing)

ISBN-10: 0692357939

Library of Congress Control Number: 2014922928

Printed In USA

Atlanta, GA

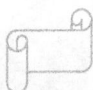

Dedicated to my father and mother

Rev. Charlie Worthen

&

Dreamal Worthen, Ph.D.

The two people who have always loved me
unselfishly☺

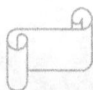

INTRODUCTION

This book has been on my heart for quite some time. I trust and pray that by the time you finish reading it, you will begin to see that there is not one single person on this planet who has the authority to abort the destiny which God has created for him or her. In fact, what is sad but true is that there are many people who go through life believing that because they may have a sordid and checkered past, God cannot use them. This is absolutely not true! God can use any person, anytime, and in any way that God so chooses. Regardless if you are a drug addict, victim of abuse, prostitute, convicted felon, homosexual, or any other societal type un-favored by people, God can use you to accomplish great and mighty things.

I am a living witness of the miraculous saving power of Jesus Christ. Throughout my life there have been many occasions where society counted me out. Society said that I would end up spending the rest of my life in prison, if not dead.

I can honestly say that if it had not been for a caring and loving father and mother, as well as a church family that would not give up praying with me and for me; society may have gotten its wish. To date I have graduated from Florida A&M University (FAMU), a prestigious historically Black College and University, with a Bachelor's Degree in Political Science and a minor in Public Administration. I have a Master of Divinity Degree (M.Div.) with honors (with a concentration in Homiletics/Worship) from The Interdenominational Theological Center Turner Seminary in Atlanta, Georgia. The M.Div. takes most students three years to complete, I completed the degree in two years. I organized a city-wide symposium entitled "Make

Your Vote Count in 2004" during the President George W. Bush and Senator John Kerry campaign. And I founded a television show called *"Carlton Worthen Presents"*, which focused on current events, as well as social and political issues.

Imagine all of this by someone who society said would never amount to anything. Look at what God can do. Look at God's grace, and God's mercy. I am not saying all of this to toot my horn or be braggadocios. I am saying this because I want you to clearly understand that where people may not be able to see the best in you, God does. Where society erects barriers and rules to block you from moving forward, God can demolish any barrier and upset any rule. People may scandalize your name and even spread vicious rumors about you. However, you must know and fully believe that God has the ability to make your enemies your footstool.

Prologue

Throughout the rest of this book we will examine the life of Jacob. We will examine the good, the bad, and the ugly. We will hone in on how from birth Jacob gave his mother Rebekah such a hard time that she had to ask God why so much pain. We will look at how God took a person who in today's society would have been rejected all because of his past. Nevertheless, God used Jacob to do awesome things that even to this day still confounds many people. Most of all, when you are done with this book you should be able to apply to your own life some of the principles that we learn from Jacob's life.

Table of Contents

Chapter 1

God Has the Final Word

> ### *God Can Use Even You*
>
> *Despite all of your issues, challenges, and flaws, God has still chosen you to carry forth a mission that has been designed just for you.*

I am ecstatic that humans don't get the final word when it comes to how God doles out blessings. I am a firm believer that if it were left to humans, only people who claim to be super spiritual and have attended church all of their lives would receive all the blessings from God. After all, the society that we live in attempts to establish who can and who cannot do certain things.

Our society says what qualifications must be met to do this and to do that. Our society determines who has the right pedigree, or who attended the right school. Society says that in order to belong to some organizations you must be of a certain socio-economic status. Society has created special boards to vet if someone is up to the organizations standards to become a part of the organization. In fact, the world in which we live does everything possible to erect barriers to keep out people that do not fit the stereotype that they feel is appropriate.

Who would have ever imagined that God would use a person named Jacob. Jacob was known to be a deceiver, a liar, a schemer, and a trickster? Who would have ever thought that God would use Jacob, who was known for manipulating so much so that he forced his older brother Esau to sell his birthright? After all, why would God not select someone who was known for always being honest? Why would God not select someone who was always known for telling the truth and not engaged in deceitful games?

You should see the looks on people's faces whenever they find out that someone does not fit the typical mold of what the ideal candidate looks like. Consider, prior to the year 2000 there was a man by the name of Barack Hussein Obama who resided in Chicago, Illinois. Obama was not even able to gain access to the Democratic National Convention in Los Angeles, California. He was denied access to the floor of the convention simply because he did not have the appropriate credentials to be in attendance to the convention.

Fast forward approximately six years later, and society continued to erect barrier after barrier against then Senator Obama as he sought the nomination to become President of the United States of America. There were evil pockets of American society who claimed that he was too radical. He was accused of hanging out with terrorists. They claimed that he was a Muslim (as if just because you are a Muslim means that you are not qualified to be a leader). And add to that the Rev. Dr. Jeremiah Wright episode that was looped on televisions across America, manipulating Americans into believing that Rev. Wright was wrong for challenging America by saying *"God damn America."*

All of this was solely because then Senator Obama did not fit the typical mold to be President of the United States of America.

For one thing, the Democratic Party already had its so called anointed leader and presumed Democratic nominee, Sen. Hillary Clinton. Secondly, he grew up in a single parent home. Finally, he did not grow up in a family that was loaded with money and/or political corporate connections. In short, now President Obama was by no means considered the ideal candidate.

In our story, we are introduced to a man by the name of Jacob. Jacob literally means heel-catcher and, trickster. For the overwhelming majority of his life Jacob developed a reputation for being as slick as a can of oil. In fact, Jacob had managed to rack up a mighty impressive vita of underhanded acts in his life. While he was in his mother Rebekah's womb he was attempting to manipulate being born first ahead of his brother Esau. Jacob's mother Rebekah shouted out as a result of the constant struggling within her womb between Jacob and Esau *"If it is to be this way, why do I live"* (Genesis 25:22).

Indeed, Jacob was what today's society would consider an unsavory person. According to society's standards, Jacob was not the ideal person who could be used by God. However, we should all be happy that humans don't have the final say so on who can and cannot be blessed by God. Yes, Jacob did cheat his brother Esau out of his birth right. Yes, Jacob did scheme with his mother Rebekah to trick his father Isaac into bestowing his blessing on him as suppose to Esau. Yes, Jacob also lied to his father Isaac when he was asked if it was really Esau he was blessing. But guess what? Despite all of Jacob's flaws and shortcomings, God still saw something in Jacob that God wanted to do. God was able to see beyond all of Jacob's shortcomings and see the good that could come out of Jacob.

In Genesis chapter 28:10-23 Jacob has a deep dream while he was at Haran. While sound asleep, God speaks to Jacob:

"I am the Lord, the God of Abraham your father, and the God of Isaac; the land on which you lie I will give to you and your offspring; and your offspring shall be like the dust of the earth, and you shall spread abroad to the west and to the east and to the north and to the south; and all families of the earth shall be blessed in you and your offspring. Know that I am with you and will keep you wherever you go, and will bring you back to this land; for I will not, leave you until I have done what I have promised you." (Genesis 28:10-15).

WOW! When Jacob awoke, he knew immediately that he had a visit from God. I mean I am sure Jacob was probably thinking surely God has the wrong guy. All the baggage Jacob had, there was no way possible that God could have really meant it. Jacob's mind was blown away by what God shared with him in his dream. Jacob says that the place he was at was awesome and that he was standing at the gate of heaven. Jacob was so ecstatic to the point that Jacob took the stone that he used as a pillow the night before and sat it up as a pillar and anointed it with oil. After anointing the stone with oil Jacob then says:

If God will be with me, and will keep me in this way that I go, and will give me bread to eat and clothing to wear so that I come again to my father's house in peace, then the Lord

shall be my God, and this stone,
which I have set up for a pillar,
shall be God's house; and of all
that You give me I will surely
give one-tenth to you (Genesis
28:16-22).

Take a moment to reflect back on a time when you just knew that it was God who had birthed something on the inside of you. Perhaps the vision was so large and so out of this world that if you dared share it with anyone they would have thought you had lost your everlasting mind. The vision could have been you heading a multi-billion dollar company. Maybe the vision was you moving out of a tiny two bed room apartment into a 5,000 square foot mansion. Or could it have been God revealing to you that you were going to be healed of a disease or sickness that doctors had given up on?

Whatever the vision may have been, it was so large and so radical you probably could not hold your peace. Or the vision was so out of this world to the point that you just knew that you would not be able to get it done because you lacked the necessary skill sets to get it done.

For Jacob this experience was so momentous that perhaps he saw flash before him all the wrong that he had ever had done in life and realized that despite of all his issues, God had chosen him for the job. That's shouting news! God has thought so much of you that despite all of your issues, challenges, and flaws, God has still chosen you to carry forth a mission that has been designed just for you.

Here's some more shouting news! Whatever it is God has revealed to you is not just for your enjoyment and pleasure alone. Notice what God told Jacob. God told Jacob that all of your offspring would be blessed as well. God is not going to just bless you. God has so many blessings that your children, and your children's children will be blessed for generations to come.

➢ *So What If You Have a Handicap?*

You must pursue with tenacity the blessings that God has for you.

The Bible is full of examples of how God has still blessed people and allowed people to grow and execute the ministries that God has called them to. God uses people despite their handicaps. I am not aware of one single person who was or is perfect other than Jesus. Yet God has an incredible record of taking imperfect people and using them mightily to accomplish kingdom work. God has proven over and over again that regardless of your handicaps God can use you.

God used Paul even though he had a thorn in his side. God used Moses even though he had a speech impediment, was a fugitive, and at times could even have a slight anger problem. Peter had such a temper that he was chopping off peoples' ears. Jeremiah could not stop crying. David had a lustful eye and a proclivity to engage in adultery. Thomas was a doubter. Noah was a drunkard. Rahab was a prostitute. What all of these people had in common was that despite their flaws, God used them mightily. These individuals were able to be used by God not because they had any super abilities, but because God was more than liberal with the grace that God poured out on them. Isn't that shouting news? With all of your flaws, with all of your handicaps, with all of the mess that's on the inside of you God still sees beyond your faults and meets your needs. It's shouting news that God still uses imperfect people to carry forward the agenda of God's kingdom.

When God makes a promise, you can bank on the promise coming to pass. All too often people allow their handicaps and lack of resources to prevent them from using what God has already blessed them with. Jacob had a faith that was unwavering that God would bring to pass that what God said God would do. Regardless of the circumstances Jacob had to face, he would not let go of the fact that God had made him a promise. This is one of the primary underpinnings of Genesis 32. Jacob is in essence reminding God that God had made a promise and because God made a promise Jacob would not let go of God until Jacob was blessed by God.

Jacob is reminding God that he would be blessed with land beyond measure in the north, south, east and west. Jacob is reminding God that he would be blessed with so many descendants that they would be uncountable. Jacob is reminding God that God promised to always be with Jacob and his descendants. In short, Jacob is communicating that he will not let go of God until the promises that have been made to him have been fulfilled. This is even if it means that Jacob will have to walk with a limp for the rest of his life.

I would much rather have a handicap and be in the will of God rather than have all the wealth in the world without a handicap and be out of the will of God. I suspect that Jacob grasped this concept regarding life. Under no circumstance should you ever allow a handicap to prevent you from pursuing the destiny that God has for you. *Do not allow your handicaps, or your short comings to be a license for you to sit back and to not pursue the promises that God has for you. You must pursue with tenacity the blessings that God has for you.*

All too often I have heard people say things such as I'm not smart enough. I'm not connected enough. I did not grow up on the right side of the tracks. I don't have enough education. I'm not with the in crowd. I don't have people to open doors for me. I don't have enough money. People use excuse after excuse after excuse. You must make the commitment right now to stop making excuses for not going after and possessing the blessings that God has for you.

➢ **God Sees Your "Not Yet"**

If people really had any idea of the fact that you are a child of God they would not handle you the way that they do. After all, people for some reason always are more inclined to see the negatives that have happened in your life rather than to keep you lifted in prayer. Rather than they see the good that God can use you for people would rather help themselves to an extra-large tub of popcorn and soda and take bets on if you will continue to stay on your back. The peanut gallery of people is literally fascinated about all of the challenges that you have to contend with. Hence, no matter how much good you may do in their eyes they are incapable of seeing the destiny that God has for you.

I have always found it very interesting that society will erect intentional barriers. The sole purpose of the barriers is to be a constant to reminder of some of the seedy and questionable things you may have done life. I mean, shucks, these same people act as if they themselves have never had any issues to contend with themselves.

Examples of issues are: generational poverty, growing up in a home without two parents. Perhaps your issue is at one time you were an adulterer. Maybe you did not have the financial resources to be able to attend college full-time. Regardless of what your issue(s) may be, people often desire to always define you by the issue(s) that you may have. Not only will people define you by your issues, they can never see the not yet that God is preparing you for.

Have you ever stopped at some point in life long enough to ask yourself this question: why are you still here? Really, as you take a moment to reflect back on where and what God has brought you through, how in the world have you been able to make it? With all of the hurts, disappointments, and rejection you are still among the land of the living. After job lay-offs, deaths of family and friends, break-ups, divorce, and sickness in your body God has seen fit for you to still be alive. Isn't that something? You are still here. May I make a suggestion of why you are still here? You are still here because God has something big for you to do. God has a special assignment that you were specifically created for. Therefore, because God has designed you for a specific task, God has also equipped you for the task. Everything you will ever need God has already divinely orchestrated for you to possess. Now it is incumbent on you to go after it.

Then Jacob awoke from his sleep and said, *"Surely the LORD is in this place—and I did not know it" (Genesis 28:16)!* Jacob himself had not fully grasped up to this point what his designed purpose in life was. When he finally realized what God had created him for he suddenly had a new bounce in his step, and a new glide in his stride. He was now a person operating in life with a new purpose. This is halleluiah shouting news! God has created **you** for a purpose!

You may feel as if you are all alone in the right now. Challenges, issues, and frustrations could be pressing and crushing you on every side. Please know that you are not crushed beyond despair. Please know that God is not relegated to just your "right now." God also knows and is shaping your future as well. That's how awesome God is. God is so awesome that God has the ability to tend to your needs in the right now, while simultaneously working everything out for your future as well: *"For surely I know the plans I have for you, says the LORD, plans for your welfare and not for harm, to give you a future with hope"(Jeremiah 29:11).*

God has a plan for you. While God may take you through wilderness situations in your life you must have the faith to believe that God is not taking you through trials to leave you, but to give you a future that is filled with hope. This is why you can rejoice even when it seems as if you will not be able to make it through your difficult times. You can shout because God is with you. You can also shout because when people look at you in your right now, you can say confidently; you may see me looking a mess now, but God is with me. You can say confidently that I don't have the house right now, but God is with me. You can say that you may not have the spouse now, but God is with me.

A lot of people can only see Jacob in his right now. God saw forty-two generations plus into the future. God saw approximately 1,680 years to the birth of Christ, and has seen approximately another 2011+ years to your "right now" and knew that God would wrap Himself in human flesh to become Jesus. Jesus would later die and be raised by God for the remission for all of humankinds sins. That's how awesome God is.

The question is whether you thank God and ask God to use you mightily to accomplish what God would have you accomplish? When you know what your specific task is that

God has created you for, will you fight against God and not pursue it? I suggest that you ask God to use you mightily.

You must also know that whatever it is God has created you for; God has not done so for only your pleasure. As we examine Jacob's story, we find that God decided to use Jacob to father the twelve tribes of Israel. Therefore, the purpose for which Jacob was created indeed benefited Jacob, but Jacob's blessing also benefited many other people in many different ways as well. You should never be under the allusion that God is blessing you for only you. God has birthed a purpose for you to also be a blessing to others as well.

Start the business God has asked you to start. Imagine how many people will benefit from what you have to offer. Imagine how many jobs you will be able to create that helps stimulate local, state, and the national economy. Imagine how many children you will be aiding by providing a job for a parent. Write that book God has asked you to write. Imagine the number of people who will be able to benefit from what God has been speaking to you. Imagine how many people will be blessed because God has blessed you.

I will not deny for one second that you may encounter difficult times while acting upon your faith to go and do what God has asked you to do. For this I suggest that you reflect on what God promised Jacob: *"Know that I am with you and will keep you wherever you go, and will bring you back to this land; for I will not leave you until I have done what I have promised you" (Genesis 28:15).*

This is what I call a blessed assurance. As you begin to straighten your back and resolve that you will walk in what God has destined for you to do you will have no reason to fear. God reminds you through His holy word that you will not be alone. Always remember that God is with you.

Take a moment right where are you are and begin to give God a radical praise for blessing you, and keeping you. Thank God for thinking enough of you to use you for a specific purpose. Declare and decree, that from this moment you will walk in the destiny that God has for you. Always remember, God sees your NOT YET.

Think About It

1. Why do you think God will overlook a persons' past to use them for God's glory?

    _____

    _____

    _____

2. Why does it seem that God often uses people to do mighty things while society says they are undesirable?

    _____

    _____

    _____

3. When you hear the name Jacob, what comes to your mind?

    _____

    _____

    _____

Reflect On It

"For I (God) will not, leave you until I have done what I have promised you"
(Genesis 28:10-15).
Pray this prayer:

Dear God,

I know that you have created me for a purpose despite what other people may think. I ask you dear God to help me to hear your voice and to walk with confidence in knowing that you will be with me every step of the way. Amen.

Action Plan

1. You have a purpose in life, therefore do not allow people to erect barriers to keep you out. Find a way to make things happen and trust that God will continue to hold you up.

2. Whenever someone tells you that you are not qualified remember, that people do not have the final word in this world, God does.

3. God does not always do things on a small scale. God does things on a big scale, so big that you will need God to accomplish it. Therefore, do not be intimidated of how big the vision is that God gives to you.

Chapter 2

You Are Valuable, So Act Like It

> ## "You Are Valuable, So Act Like It"

Never Underestimate Your Value!

Another important lesson we can all learn from Jacob is how he was able to see beyond the immediate and grasp the concept of planning for the long road ahead. In life if not yourself, you may know of people who seem to appreciate the fact that you must plan today in order to live for tomorrow. Jacob clearly understood planning for the road ahead.

Jacob had the uncanny ability to understand that the culture in which he lived, the birth right was something to be adored. His brother Esau saw the birthright as worth only one meal. In fact, Esau had such reckless disregard... short minded and lacking in business acumen... that he willingly sold his birthright for the one meal.

This sounds like so many people today in the 21st century. Instead of looking and preparing for the long road ahead, they would rather have immediate gratification today instead. Esau had no clue or respect of the value and privileges that came with being a first-born son in his culture.

Once when Jacob was cooking a stew, Esau came in from the field, and he was famished. Esau said to Jacob, "Let me eat some of that red stuff, for I am famished!" (Therefore he was called Edom.) Jacob said, "First sell me your birthright." Esau said, "I am about to die; of what use is a birthright to me?" Jacob said, "Swear to me first." So he swore to him, and sold his birthright to Jacob. Then Jacob gave Esau bread and lentil stew, and he ate and drank, and rose and went his way. Thus Esau despised his birthright (Genesis 25:29-34).

How many people do you know who allowed one night of pleasure to entice them to the point that they made a serious error in judgment? By not having a since of the value that God has placed in you and on you, if you are not careful you will literally render your value valueless if allowed. Making poor decisions has the potential to wreak unbelievable hardship in your life if you do not place a value on what God has so richly blessed you with. This is an extremely important concept that must be understood: *never underestimate the value that you are and that you have.*

Your value derives from the fact that God has invested so much in you. Consider, God created you unlike anyone else on this earth. You are one of a kind... that's value. God has redeemed you from many dangers, toils, and snares, that's value. God has allowed you to be able to keep your sanity while in insane situations, that's value. I could go on and on. Because God has invested so much into you, it is incumbent upon you to never compromise the value that God has on you.

You are incredibly valuable in God's eyes regardless of your past. Regardless of what other people may think about you, you are valuable. You are valuable because you are fearfully and wonderfully made in the image of God. You are God's child. Because you are God's child, you should not allow any person or devil in hell to make you feel invaluable. You are so valuable in God's eyes that God knows the number of hairs that are on your head. Now that you know you are a person of immense value, do not allow people to diminish your value with their harsh words.

➢ **Don't Digest**

Has there been a point in your life where you have received body blows that were so devastating that the impact of the punches almost brought you to your knees? What is even more alarming is that often times body blows that you receive in life can even come from people who are closest to you. These body blows are not inflicted by a physical hand; they are inflicted by a person's mouth.

Words can also be viewed in my opinion as a diet. For example, there is nothing wrong with a slice of pizza. However, if you eat pizza three hundred sixty-five days a year, three times a day, it is quite likely you will begin to suffer from some dietary complications. Just as you should not eat pizza every day of the week three times a day you must not allow people to feed you with words that are intentionally designed to cause you harm and to break your spirit.

You may not be able to control what people say about you. Yes, there are also people who cannot stand to see your face, not because you have said or done anything. There may also be people who simply cannot stand to see the anointing and the call that God has on your life. Therefore, these same people will resort to talking about you, scandalizing your name, and calling you every name but a child of God. Child of God you can shout, sing, and give God praise in the midst of your *haters* serving up harmful foods because you are still anointed.

While you are anointed, and while people may not be able to stand the anointing that is on your life you still have a move that no devil in hell can stop you from making. The move is you do not have to digest the poisonous food that is being served. You do not have to be fazed or discouraged by their words because at the end of the day your *haters* have absolutely no control over the call, and the destiny that God has for you. Remember, God knew you before you were ever conceived in your mother's womb: *"For surely I know the plans I have for you, says the LORD, plans for your welfare and not for harm, to give you a future with hope" (Jeremiah 29:11).*

What people do not understand is that God's word alone is all that matters. For some reason, a lot of people have it all wrong. People feel that they have the last word. People feel that their word alone can stop and start things if God has already ordained things to happen. When God speaks, worlds are formed. When God speaks, oceans are formed. When God speaks, human races are made. When God speaks, order is made out of chaotic situations.

> *So shall my word be that goes out from my mouth; it shall not return to me empty, but it shall accomplish that which I purpose, and succeed in the thing for which I sent it (Isaiah 55:11).*

Please do not digest the negative words that people will hurl at you. Do not allow people to use your past to cause you to feel guilty about the call that God has for you. God equipped you before the foundations of the earth were even created. God spoke into your life before your ancestors were ever created. Now that God has spoken, there is not one thing a human can do to stop or block you.

You should be rejoicing right now that God gets the final say so. Whereas people have levied severe body blows through words against you in life, thank God that they did not have the ability to prevent you from walking in the destiny that God has for you. Thank God that when God speaks His word will accomplish what it has been sent forth to do.

When you look at Jacob's life, regardless of how people may feel towards him, one thing was certain. Jacob was undoubtedly chosen by God for a specific purpose. Because Jacob was chosen by God there was absolutely nothing that anyone could do to stop him from accomplishing what God had already ordained before Jacob was ever born.

My friend, settle in your saddle, and square your shoulders. God has already spoken into and over your life. Your *haters* and enemies have all made one crucial mistake with the negative diet of words they have attempted to feed you. It is that same diet of words that drives you to your knees day in and day out for God to be with you. Keep your head up as you walk in the destiny that God has called you to: *"If God will be with me, and will keep me in this way that I go, and will give me bread to eat and clothing to wear so that I come again to my father's house in peace, then the Lord shall be my God" (Genesis 28:20-21).*

Think About It

1. Why are people always determined to never see others for the potential that they have as supposed to always keeping them confined to their past?

_____

_____

_____

2. What has stopped or is stopping you from relentlessly pursuing what God has created you for?

_____

_____

_____

3. Why should you rejoice whenever challenging situations arise while you are pursuing what God has created you for?

_____

_____

_____

Reflect On It

"For surely I know the plans I have for you, says the LORD, plans for your welfare and not for harm, to give you a future with hope" (Jeremiah 29:11).

Pray this prayer:

Dear God,

There are many people who desire to keep me confined to my past. Please give me the clarity as well as the patience to know that despite my past, you have big plans for my future. Amen.

Action Plan

God has brought you a long way. You cannot stop now on the path that God has created you for. Keep moving, keep praying, and remember that part of your blessing is to bless others as well.

1. Start today and write down the necessary steps that are necessary for you to begin on the path that God has created you for.

2. Get a new bounce in your step and a new glide in your stride right now and begin to operate your life with purpose! What can you do?

Chapter 3

So What If You Have A Past, Who Doesn't?

Everyone Is Not Happy To See You Grow

Haters can't stand to see that God is blessing you beyond your wildest dreams.

At the beginning of my ministry, there was a certain individual who seemed to be determined to stifle it from starting, not to mention that once the ministry started he did all he could to smear my name. I have learned in life that whenever you are ready to step from under someone else's shadow, they will not always be happy to see you grow. I must be honest with you, I get excited when people begin to try to block me from walking in the destiny that God has for me. If I could borrow a page from street language, these people are what I call haters. A *hater* is anyone who despises the fact that God has decided to favor you.

A person who tries to block you or who is a *hater* will stay up late at night while everyone else is sound asleep plotting and devising ways to prevent you from walking in the overflow blessings that God has your name on. These same people will smile in your face, eat with you, and pat you on your back. When it comes time for you to spread your own wings, they will do everything they can to throw up road blocks in an effort to stunt your growth. Yet through all of the unnecessary drama, you should always know that God is with you!

David was well aware that even though *haters* will come, they will not be able to abort the destiny that God has for you. That's shouting news there! Your haters and blockers cannot abort the destiny that God has for you.

David hit the nail right on the head: *"You prepare a table before me in the presence of my enemies; You anoint my head with oil; my cup overflows" (Psalm 23:5).*

What gets me excited about people who are blockers and *haters* is that God will elevate you right in their face. When God elevates you there is not one thing any hater or any blocker can do to prevent you from continuing to move forward in life.

This happened to Jacob as well. Jacob worked for his uncle Laban for twenty years. For fourteen of the twenty years he pursued Rachel in order to marry her. Seven years he agreed to work for his uncle Laban in order to be able to marry Rachel. When the seven years (Genesis 29:18) were up and there was a grand wedding, Laban deceived Jacob by allowing Rachel's sister Leah to be the person to consummate the marriage. Obviously, Jacob was greatly disappointed. Laban had deceived Jacob and has now manipulated the situation for Jacob to work for another seven years (Genesis 29: 20) in order to be able to marry the woman that Jacob really loved.

To exacerbate things more, Jacob continued to work for Laban all in an effort to demonstrate his love and desire to marry Rachel: *"These twenty years I have been with you; your ewes and your female goats have not miscarried, and I have not eaten the rams of your flocks" (Genesis 31:38).*

Jacob worked in the most arduous of conditions. Freezing cold, blistering heat, and torrential rainstorms... Jacob was loyal to Laban. For nearly two decades (don't forget the fourteen years he desired to marry Rachel) Laban benefited from the savvy business acumen, loyalty, wisdom, and knowledge that God bestowed upon Jacob. For nearly two decades, Jacob grew the net worth of Laban's stock portfolio. Laban had little before Jacob arrived to seek refuge at uncle Laban's estate.

I can imagine what Jacob must have said to his uncle Laban, Now listen, the time has come for my family and I to launch out on our own. Uncle Laban we have been with you for quite a few years now. I have made you a very wealthy man. Your bank account is phat beyond your wildest dreams. When I arrived here you had almost nothing. Now look at what you have.

Laban replies, to Jacob: *"If you will allow me to say so, I have learned by divination that the LORD has blessed me because of you; name your wages, and I will give it" (Genesis 30:27-29).*

Laban knew full well the contribution that Jacob had made to his household. Now that Jacob desires to go and make an estate for him and his family, Laban begins to become indignant. As you read the story in its entirety, you also learn that once Jacob shared his desire to move on in life, Laban threw up road block after road block to stymie Jacob's progress.

Laban even went as far as intentionally tampering with all of the livestock that he owned because he knew that Jacob had the ability to be successful at whatever he set his hand to do. Hence, Laban intentionally did everything possible to cause Jacob to fail in his attempt to leave the house of Laban with what was really due to him.

At some point in our lives, we all have found ourselves in some situations and wondered why in the world we were taken advantage of. There has been some supervisor who has made the work place an unbearable place to work in. Perhaps it's a spouse who never appreciates what you have to offer. There may even be people who seem to not care or choose to acknowledge the gifts that you bring to ministry.

There are quite a few lessons that can be learned from Jacob's dealings with his uncle Laban. One lesson is that even though Jacob was in an undesirable situation he was still loyal to Laban. Through all of the treachery, through all of the unfairness that Laban inflicted upon Jacob, Jacob remained loyal. Not once did Jacob speak ill of Laban. Not once did Jacob not complete what was asked of him.

Throughout the ordeal, God continued to allow Laban to prosper as well as Jacob. God continued to meet every need that Jacob had. God demands that we also have the same outlook when it comes to our work. Regardless of how trying the situation may be, if God has placed you there, do the job that is expected of you. God will honor you; and in due season, God will also exalt you. Please notice that I did not write if you placed yourself there; I wrote if *God places you there*.

The second lesson we can learn from Jacobs's dealings with Laban is that Jacob understood the importance of seasons. Jacob was very aware that if he tried to operate under his own intellect and devices he very well could have failed. Jacob knew that although Laban was not what he regarded as ideal, God had Jacob to stay at Laban's for a season. The unfortunate thing about seasons is we never know how long a season may be. Nevertheless, you must be obedient to where and what God has you doing. Your season for elevation will come. Your season to move to the next chapter in your life will come. What Jacob teaches us is that there is absolutely nothing you can do to rush the seasons. All you can do is to continue to stay prayed up. For if you operate *out of your season you will fail.*

Solomon was correct when he penned the following words regarding seasons:

For everything there is a season, and a time for every matter under heaven: *a time to be born, and a time to die; a time to plant, and a time to pluck up what is planted; a time to kill, and a time to heal; a time to break down, and a time to build up...;* (Ecclesiastes 3:1-3).

The third lesson we can learn from Jacob is how God will take His time at developing you to become what God will have you to become. Let's face it, when God begins to develop and strengthen you it is never fun. God worked on Jacob for nearly two decades before God was through with him. During that two decades plus ordeal, God taught Jacob character, what it means to be committed, as well as how it feels to be deceived.

Please do not think it was ironic that the master deceiver himself was in a situation where he had finally grown tired of being tricked, lied to, and taken for a fool by his uncle Laban. Now that the shoe was on the other foot Jacob had a good dose of his own medicine. After all, there is an old saying that is also a biblical truth: *"Do not be deceived; God is not mocked, for you reap whatever you sow" (Galatians 6:7).* Not only did Jacob receive a dose of his own medicine, more importantly Jacob had the opportunity to mature in learning how to interact with people. This is another irony in how God teaches people lessons in life. God will place you in situations where your desire may be for God to get you out of the situation. You may be totally unaware that God is actually allowing you to go through the difficult situations all in an effort to prepare you for blessings that are yet to come.

In short, this is why it is important that you not despise the people who may come into your life and begin to get on your last nerve. That person may be a spouse, co-worker, member of your church... it very well could be that same person who is being used by God to teach you life lessons such as patience, longsuffering, industriousness, loyalty, and faithfulness.

The fourth lesson we can learn from Jacob's interaction with Laban is mercy. Jacob knew that he had serious issues with his character. He also knew that his brother Esau was greatly upset and angry with the fact that he was tricked out of his birthright and tricked his father Isaac into giving him Esau's blessing. To compound things even more, Laban resorted to duplicitous means in order to trick Jacob by tampering with the way Laban's sheep were raised.

Yet through all of this, God still blessed Jacob. WOW! God still blessed Jacob despite all of the wrong that Jacob had done. This is what is called grace and mercy. God showed mercy to Jacob rather than judgment. How many people do you know would bless someone after they have intentionally deceived them, tricked them, and taken advantage of them? God will.

Despite all of Jacob's shortcomings, God still blessed and prospered Jacob with financial wealth, children, wives, and land. So, the next time you begin to become irritated and want to throw in the towel because of people mistreating and taking advantage of you, always remember that God is preparing you for an even bigger blessing.

In no way am I suggesting that you simply lie down and allow people to steamroll you. What I am saying is that if you ever expect to walk in the overflow blessings of God, you will have to learn how to as the prophet Micah says Micah: *"treat people with mercy, kindness, justice and always remember to walk humbly with God" (Micah 6:8).*

➢ You Can't Be Blocked

When God elevates you there is not one thing any hater or any blocker can do to prevent you from continuing to move forward in life!

I had to save this final lesson we can learn from Jacob's interaction with Laban. The lesson is that there is absolutely nothing anyone can do to block you from walking in the blessings that God has just for you. A sad truth is that contrary to how you may feel, there will be people who will come into your life for the expressed purpose to cause you stress upon stress. Even with all of the unnecessary drama and stress, God sees what you are going through.

Take a moment where you are and begin to celebrate, that even though you may be in an undesirable situation, God is still with you. God is developing you, maturing you, but most of all prospering you. Praise God for being ever so merciful towards you. Celebrate God moving you from one glory to the next. Celebrate God still continuing to allow you to be blessed beyond your wildest dreams, even though there are people who cannot stand to see you blessed. Celebrate and thank God for preparing you for the new season that you are being prepared for.

You can rest when people begin to try and block you in life. You can rest and enjoy a nice glass of lemonade in the shade because it is not you yourself who is keeping you; it is the Lord who is keeping you. Isn't that good to know? You don't have to keep yourself from the plots, schemes, and tricks of your haters and blockers, the Lord will keep you. Take a look at what one Psalmist had to say about people who are up to nothing but causing evil: *"The LORD will keep you from all evil; He will keep your life. The LORD will keep your going out and your coming in from this time on and forevermore" (Psalm 121:7-8)*.

Not only will the Lord keep you from all evil, but the Lord has another way of dealing with your haters and blockers also. The Lord will not allow anything that is fashioned to do you harm to be successful. When your enemies rise up against you, simply reflect on what the prophet Isaiah was told: *"No weapon that is fashioned against you shall prosper, and you shall confute every tongue that rises against you in judgment. This is the heritage of the servants of the LORD and their vindication from me, says the Lord" (Isaiah 54:17)*.

Jacob was indeed going through a bout of hater-aide being poured all over him by his uncle Laban. However, because God is all seeing, and all knowing God had an angel to visit Jacob while he was asleep. Did you notice what I just said? Jacob is sound asleep, while Laban is plotting and devising the fall and demise of Jacob. When you keep your hand in God's hand you will begin to have sweet rest when there is confusion and chaos all around you. Take a look at what the angel shared with Jacob:

> *Then the angel of God said*
> *to me in the dream, 'Jacob,' and*
> *I said, 'Here I am!' And he said,*
> *'Look up and see that all the*
> *goats that leap on the flock are*
> *striped, speckled, and mottled;*

for I have seen all that Laban is doing to you. I am the God of Bethel, where you anointed a pillar and made a vow to me. Now leave this land at once and return to the land of your birth.' Then Rachel and Leah answered him, 'Is there any portion or inheritance left to us in our father's house? Are we not regarded by him as foreigners? For he has sold us, and he has been using up the money given for us. All the property that God has taken away from our father belongs to us and to our children; now then, do whatever God has said to you' (Genesis 31:11-18).

Not only did God protect Jacob, but God also addressed the fact that God was aware of how Laban had mistreated him, as well as his daughters. God spoke to Laban and told him that the time had now come for he and his family to move forward. What's even more exciting is that God did not send Jacob away from Laban empty handed. On top of that, two sisters who were earlier in competition with each other are now working together because of the evil that was perpetrated against them as well. Isn't God good?

Take a moment and let's shout together! Your haters and blockers can't stop you. Celebrate that while your blockers and haters are up at night, you can get a good night's sleep. Give

God praise that every weapon that is formed against you will not prosper.

Think About It

1. According to the chapter reading, define what a "hater" is?

   _____

   _____

   _____

2. How should you handle haters in your life?

   _____

   _____

   _____

3. What are some of the lessons in life that Jacob should have learned from Laban?

   _____

   _____

   _____

Reflect On It

"These twenty years I have been with you; your ewes and your female goats have not miscarried, and I have not eaten the rams of your flocks" (Genesis 31:38).

Dear God,

Please give me the strength to be able to do what is right even when people conspire against me. Please continue to grant me favor even when I am in undesirable situations. Amen.

Action Steps

You will always have to contend with haters in your life. It is important for you to remember that regardless of you may feel, your haters will not win as long as you continue to pursue the destiny that God has for you.

1. Smile when your haters conspire against you. God is preparing you for something big.
2. Remember, God is not mocked. Therefore, continue to do what is right and God will honor you.

Chapter 4

Let the Past Be the Past

Do not allow people to raise up your past to prevent you from being able to walk in the blessings that God has for you.

Under no circumstance should you ever allow people to use your past against you. This happens all too often in life. I often share the story of an individual who did everything he could to use my past against me to prevent me from starting in my ministry. This individual told me in his office one day that as long as he had anything to do with me moving forward in ministry, it would never happen. This same individual took it upon himself to begin throwing up my past against me. Not only did he throw up my past with the two of us privately, but he then proceeded to do the same publically as well.

He would throw up how I was such an unsavory person in the past. He also reminded me that because of the past it would be a stumbling block for other people. These people would not desire to have someone who had the scars and bruises I had to serve as their pastor and/or lead them in any type of ministry. In other words, what this individual was implying was that he was now God.

Beloved, don't you know if I had listened to this person, and received what this person was speaking into my life, I very well may not be here today! I very well could be fumbling and stumbling through life not walking out the divine call and plan that God has on my life.

Just as this happened to me, I am certain that this has happened with you also. I am certain that there have been people who have told you that you are not smart enough. Perhaps there have been people who have said that your momma wasn't anything, your dad was a deadbeat, and that you do not know what you are doing. Perhaps someone has told you that you are the laughing stock of the city. Listen: ***Do not allow people to raise up your past to prevent you from being able to walk in the blessings that God has for you.***

As we look at Jacob wrestle and tussle with God, God in essence asks Jacob a rhetorical question. God asked Jacob what his name was: *So he said to him, "What is your name?" And he said, "Jacob." Then the man said, "You shall no longer be called Jacob, but Israel, for you have striven with God and with humans, and have prevailed" (Genesis 32:27-28).*

You may not have been in church all of your life. You may not be able to recite all of the books of the Bible in order from Genesis to Revelation. You may not even be that eloquent of a speaker. However, you are aware that God is all knowing, and all seeing. Therefore, why in the world would God ask a question for which God clearly already knew the answer?

God asked Jacob the rhetorical question not because God did not know the answer. God asked Jacob what his name was so that Jacob could see who he really was. God brought before Jacob his name so that once God caused a change in Jacob's life; Jacob would know that only God has the power to change someone's name. In other words, the implication by God was,

Jacob do you see the type person you are? Do you see that you have constantly fought against your brother? Do you not see that you were a thief and a manipulator? Have you not used all types of trickery and deceit? Have you not been duplicitous, and cunning only to try and get ahead in life? Jacob because you have done this I cannot bless you.

That's not God's attitude towards Jacob. The only thing God was showing Jacob is that is who he used to be. God wants Jacob to know that because he has wrestled and striven with God. God found it pleasing that Jacob would not let him go until he saw brought to pass the blessings that God had promised him. It was at this point that God removed Jacob's old name and gave him a new name called Israel.

In other words, there will come a time in your life when you begin to seek God's face to change you for the better. Not only will you desire for God to make a change in your life, but you will have a sincere desire to have God's will be acted out as well. This is when God will begin to work in you and through you. God will change your name when you begin to yield to God's moving in your life.

The people who knew you from your past will not be able to recognize you when God gets through with you. That's another shouting point right there! Don't take my word that God can use you even with your horrific past. Take a look at a few examples of people in the Bible who had unsavory pasts yet God still used them for His glory.

Moses was known for his speech impediment. He also was a murderer as well as a fugitive. But when he had an encounter with God, Moses became a liberator and a leader who walked and talked with authority who led the Israelites out of Egypt.

Saul had an encounter with Jesus on the Damascus road. Saul went from being a persecutor and accomplice to the murder of Stephen to being credited with writing over half of the New Testament books and epistles in the Holy Bible.

And look at what has happened with Jacob! He used to be called heel-catcher, trickster, conniver, and schemer. In Genesis Chapter 32 Jacob is being blessed by God. In short, do not allow people to speak negative words into your life. God says in His holy word that you are the head and not the tail. You are blessed in the city, and blessed in the field. God says that if you would diligently seek Him, He will show Himself to you. God's word says that for whosoever will, let them come.

Declare today that under no circumstances will you allow anyone to talk you out of the blessings that God has for you. Make the commitment today that from now on, no one will be able to sow seeds of doubt into your mind. Decree that as long as you have breath in your body no one will ever be able to use your past against you.

God asked Jacob what his name was. God brought to the forefront that Jacob had a seedy past. But guess what? We have all done some questionable and seedy things in life. The only difference for some is that they were caught and everything was put on public display for the world to see. For others they were able to get away with it and perhaps no one else knows about it. But guess what? God knows every little thing you have done in life, the good as well as the bad. God knows that person you slept with outside of your covenant marriage. God knows how you have deceived and defrauded the company you may work for. God knows the ill will and the intent that is in your heart towards your neighbor. God even knows the selfish desires that you may have deep down in your own heart.

God does not hold any of this against you. God will allow those situations to come to your forefront so that God will be able to show you how merciful He is. People are not always merciful, but God is merciful. God is a God of such infinite grace and mercy. Where people will allow the past to be brought up in front of you, and used to belittle and hold you back, God will use those same circumstances and situations to dust you off and, cleanse you, remind you that you are His child. Because you are God's child, you can walk in the blessings that He has for you. Take a moment right where you are and begin to give God praise for thinking enough of you to not continue to use your past to beat you down or hold you back! Instead, God pours out grace upon grace, and mercy upon mercy on you. God strengthens and empowers you to be able to walk with authority, even if it's with a limp from wrestling with God.

Therefore, when someone comes to you and says "I remember you when," you can reply "Yeah, but God knows me and God had cleansed me. God has made me whole and I can now walk in the blessings of God with my head held high."

➢ *Don't Allow the Past to Intimidate You*

Please know that just because God leads you from an unsavory place does not always mean that your past will not begin to relentlessly pursue you. Your past will make every effort to detract you from your destiny. You have to determine that although you are in route to a destination, you will not allow any person or anything to deter you from reaching it.

Recall earlier in the chapter I shared with you that Jacob had made up his mind that he was ready to leave his uncle Laban's estate and begin to establish an estate for his own family. This was news that Laban was not pleased to hear. Nevertheless,

Jacob along with his family, decided to leave anyway (Laban had no clue that Jacob had left).

Laban learned approximately three days after the fact that Jacob and his entire family had finally left Laban's estate. This greatly infuriated him, so much so that he immediately dropped everything he was doing to pursue Jacob. Keep in mind, Jacob and his family had a three-day head start on Laban. Nevertheless, Laban could not stomach the fact that not only had Jacob and his family left Laban, but Jacob did not leave empty handed.

Laban was finally able to catch up with Jacob in a period of his journey towards his homeland at a place called Gilead, which in the Hebrew means "rugged." Not only was Gilead a rugged terrain, but it was also a mountainous terrain. Isn't that interesting? Jacob is in route to his destination and right when he is in the thick and the most challenging leg of the journey his past catches up with him in an attempt to derail his destination.

What's also interesting about Gilead is that this area near Palestine was known for its heavy forest. Therefore, it was an excellent place for people to hide out who were on the run from people pursuing them. Jacob is on the run from Laban, yet Jacob was clear about his instructions from God: *"Return to the land of your ancestors and to your kindred, and I will be with you" (Genesis 31:3)*. There was no mistake about it; the Lord was crystal clear that the time had come for Jacob to move away from Laban.

What's also worth pointing out about Gilead is that this is the same place David sought refuge from his son, Absalom, when he was pursuing David to kill him. The Israelites' sought refuge in Gilead from the Philistines as well. Gilead was also known for its tributaries, water, and good land for livestock to eat from. That's God for you. God will lead you through a densely forested territory that can be difficult to navigate, yet God will provide you with enough substance that you are not in lack for anything.

You may not have everything you want in life; however, God still makes a way out of no way and is still in the business of making the seemingly impossible possible. God made it possible for Jacob, his family, and all of the livestock to be able to lie down in green pastures, in a mountainous and dense forest area, and yet be led by the still waters as well. There must be some truth to the comment of David: *"I've never seen the righteous forsaken, or God's seed beg bread" (Psalm 37:25).*

What is also worth pointing out is that as Jacob is in route to a destination where he may have thought that he had finally escaped his past with uncle Laban. Of course, this was not the case. You should know that Jacob had a three-day head-start on Laban before he was even aware that Jacob had left the estate. In the end it took Laban a total of ten days to catch up to Jacob. This, my friend is worth us taking a moment to explore this interesting phenomenon.

Often times in life you may have resolved within yourself that enough is enough and you will begin to pursue the destiny that God has created you for. The mistake that a lot of people make is that they are under the false illusion that just because God has birthed a vision in them or instructed them to move from one season in their life to another, that their past will choose to stay in the past. This is not so. Please understand that your past will pursue you mercilessly until it finds you.

Just because your past begins to pursue you does not mean that you should walk in fear. The question becomes how will you respond when your past catches up with you? Will you tuck your tail and run? Will you coward up and capitulate to the abuse of your past? Will you allow your past to talk you out of the journey that you are on? Only you can make these decisions.

What you must know about your past is that your past often times has one purpose. The one primary purpose of someone constantly leveling assault upon assault against you with your past is an effort to make you feel ugly, inadequate, and incapable of pursuing and walking in the destiny that God has for you. At this juncture in your life you must remain resolute in knowing that God has been with you through many dangers, toils and snares. You must know beyond the shadow of a doubt that God will complete the delivery process of delivering you from current and future storms, which in this case is your past.

What you do when your past finally catches up to you is vitally important. I suggest that you stare your past right square in the eye and trust that God will carry you through. Tell your past that you are thankful for the reminder of what and who you use to be. Do this regardless of how good or bad the past may be. Tell the past that if it was not for the past you never would have been able to see God's mighty and tender hand protecting you despite the desire your past had to crush you to nothingness.

Take a deep breath, and inhale all of God and God's Godness. Exhale the past and watch it go bye-bye. Reflect and meditate on where and what God has brought you from to where God has now brought you to. But don't stop there! Also reflect and meditate on where God is taking you to.

I submit that when you are clear on issues and situations that God has delivered you from that there will be no devil in hell that can bring up your past to manipulate, bully, and intimidate you.

Think About It

1. Take a moment and share how people have used your past against you.

   _____

   _____

   _____

2. How did you feel when someone used your past against you?

   _____

   _____

   _____

3. Why is it important for you to stare your past in the eye and speak directly to your past?

   _____

   _____

   _____

4. What do you think your life would be like if God decided to always hold your past against you?

   _____

   _____

   _____

5. Relate Gilead to a time in your life when you had left your past, but your past caught up to you?

   _____

   _____

   _____

Reflect On It

"So he said to him, 'What is your name?' And he said, 'Jacob.' Then the man said, You shall no longer be called Jacob, but Israel, for you have striven with God and with humans, and have prevailed"(Genesis 32:27-28).

Pray this prayer:

Dear God,

I thank you for my past. I thank you for delivering me from my past. Thank you for not allowing the past to consume me to the point that it killed me. Now God, I pray that just as you have brought me to this point in my life that you will continue to be with me as you take me from one glory to the next. Amen.

Action Plan

1. Speak directly to your past and tell it today is the last day that it will have any authority over you.

2. Walk with and in authority in the destiny that God has for you, and declare no devil in hell can ever use your past against you again.

3. God has given you a new name, now act like you have a new name.

Chapter 5

Prayer Is Essential

> ➢ **Prayer Life**

There is no need to trip and flip out because you find yourself in a challenging situation!

Jacob knew very well that his prayer life with God was essential for him to be able to operate on a day to day basis. Jacob knew that if he was not involved intimately with God he quite well would have fallen flat on his face. A sad truth for many people is that prayer is the last thing on their mind. Don't get me wrong, I'm aware that people will throw at God a quick request whenever they want God to do something for them. This was not Jacob's habit. Jacob had a habit of being in constant communication with God. When you take a close look at the prayer Jacob offered to God you can clearly see that Jacob indeed had an intimate relationship with God. Jacob knew that God had proven to be faithful with honoring His promises. Jacob also knew that he could take his concerns and fears directly to God as well.

Unfortunately for many people the only time they will bend their knees to pray is when they are drenched in the coat of fear. The fear may be a challenging time in your life. Perhaps the fear is a pressing financial matter; maybe the fear is a grim diagnosis you have received from a doctor. Fear will push you to enter into prayer like never before, especially if you find yourself unemployed and you have no money flowing into your home, but you have bills stacked sky high.

I can honestly say that there have been times in my own personal life where things have become so stressful to the point where I was driven to my knees. Life has a way of causing you to be so afraid to the point that you cannot sleep. A lackluster prayer life may cause you to become irritable, and your conversations become all consuming on the issue that seems bigger than you. Life can place you smack in the middle of what I call a pressure cooker. If I can sum it up in one word about how life can be, that word would "be stressful." Jacob was in a stressful situation.

Jacob received a message that his "D-Day" was quickly approaching. "D-Day" for Jacob was that he would have to see his brother Esau, who he had wronged face to face. Jacob knew that the last time he had laid eyes on Esau was when Esau had desired to kill him for the wrongs that had been inflicted upon him by his brother. Certainly, this had to be a stressful situation for Jacob.

Often times when people find themselves in stressful situations they seem to develop amnesia of exactly who God is. There is no need to trip and flip out because you find yourself in a challenging situation. Challenges and hostile situations are all a part of life. Challenges and hostile situations are tests that will assess your maturity in faith and exactly how much you trust God to show up and do the impossible. If anyone had reason to be fearful and stressed out, Jacob did. Don't get me wrong. I am not implying that fear is not something that is genuine. Fear is indeed something that must be properly handled. How you handle your fears, challenges, and hostile situations is critically important. Take a moment and examine how Jacob handled his fear when he knew that his brother had one thing on his mind regarding Jacob, and that was to kill him.

First, Jacob realized that everything he had and everything he was had nothing to do with him being so much smarter than anyone else. Jacob understood that the only reason that he was still alive and that he had any measure of wealth was because God had been with him throughout his life. Jacob knew that if he had to rely on his own devices he would have been devoured by Esau a long time ago. If Esau had not devoured him surely his uncle Laban would have done so. However, because of God's infinite grace and mercy no harm was brought to Jacob.

> *And Jacob said, "O God of my father Abraham and God of my father Isaac, O LORD who said to me, 'Return to your country and to your kindred, and I will do you good,' I am not worthy of the least of all the steadfast love and all the faithfulness that you have shown to your servant, for with only my staff I crossed this Jordan; and now I have become two companies. Deliver me, please, from the hand of my brother, from the hand of Esau, for I am afraid of him; he may come and kill us all, the mothers with the children. Yet you have said, 'I will*

surely do you good, and make your offspring as the sand of the sea, which cannot be counted because of their number' " (Genesis 32:7-12).

Second, Jacob leads off his prayer acknowledging that without God's steadfast love and faithfulness surely failure would have come. We can learn a lot from this simple prayer. You can learn that when you approach God, you do not always have to approach God with your hands out, but with your hands up.

When you approach God with your hands up, what you are saying is "God the situations I am facing are too unbearable for me to handle on my own. The weight of the problems will crush me without your divine help and intervention." When you approach God with your hands up you are implying to God that you have done all that you can humanly do and that you are now in need of God's super to meet your natural in order for supernatural things to happen. **Trust me, Jacob needed for God to do a supernatural act in his life.**

Third, Jacob had no problem admitting to God that he was scared out of his everlasting mind. Jacob said to God *"Deliver me, please, from the hand of my brother, from the hand of Esau, for I am afraid of him" (Genesis 32:11).* Jacob points out for you that there is absolutely nothing wrong with telling God that you are afraid. What this means is that you are able to approach God with any care and concern you may have. Once you approach God with your cares and concerns you can then rest comfortably in the bosom of God and know that everything will be alright. *"Cast all your anxiety on him, because he cares for you" (1 Peter 5:7).*

➢ Prayer is a Direct Link

Prayer for a person of faith is the essential direct link with God. For every person that is growing in faith, I can show you a person who has an active prayer life.

All too often, individuals treat prayer as if it is only a monologue with God. Prayer is much more than this. If you are ever going to walk in the overflow blessings that God has in store for you, it will be essential that you treat prayer as a dialogue with God instead. This is a foundational premise that will play a foundational role in developing a close an intimate relationship with God. Therefore, I encourage you to begin developing a strong and vibrant prayer life today. After all, there is an old saying, "little prayer, little power, much prayer, much power."

Yes, praying is when you make your request known to God. However, prayer is also an opportunity for God to speak to you as well. I encourage you the next time you pray to not be in such a hurry to say "Amen", and rush off to whatever it is you have to do. You will be amazed at how God will begin to reveal Himself to you in those moments of silence and solitude. You will be amazed at how chaotic moments will become much clearer as you begin to hear the voice of God begin to guide you in whatever situation you may be in.

I recall a time in my ministry when I had an opportunity to pastor a church that was approximately four hours from Atlanta, Georgia where my wife and I currently reside. I was excited that I was even considered to pastor the church. As I began to consider if this was indeed an opportunity that should be explored I began to converse with people who were close to me. I talked with my wife and she made her concerns known. She shared with me what she saw as the pros as well as the cons. I shared with her as well what I considered the pros and the cons were. I spoke with two of my seminary classmates for their input. Their input was that there would be unlimited potential once I made the move and that it would be quite possible that I would be seen as a future leader within my denomination. My two friends also shared with me that if I made the move my ministry career would be on the fast track as well.

I cannot begin to tell you the amount of sleep I lost in trying to decide if I should take this pastoral opportunity. I began to notice that the only thing that was on my mind morning, noon, and night was to make the right decision. Of course things were not made easy for me, considering that at the time my wife was also in the application stage of applying to seminary as well, in addition to nearly completing her first Master's Degree. I was a wreck.

It was not until my father and I began to discuss the issue and he shared with me that I needed to settle myself down and pray to God about the entire situation. That was what was missing; I did not have peace because I had not spent enough quality time with God on the issue. When I began to seek God's face regarding the decision that had to be made my chaotic world suddenly became less chaotic and sleeping at night was no longer a problem. Paul says that we should never worry about anything, but we should take all of our concerns to God:

> *Do not worry about anything, but in everything by prayer and supplication with thanksgiving let your requests be made known to God. And the peace of God, which surpasses all understanding,*

will guard your hearts and your minds
in Christ Jesus (Philippians 4:6-7).

Think About It

1. Why is prayer essential for maintaining an intimate relationship with God?

_____

_____

_____

2. List as many benefits as you can that derive from an active prayer life?

_____

_____

_____

3. How do you feel after you have spent time in prayer with God?

_____

_____

_____

4. How did Jacob handle the fear he had regarding his brother Esau?

_____

_____

_____

5. When approaching God in prayer with your hands up, what does this signify in the reading?

_____

_____

_____

Reflect On It

"Deliver me, please, from the hand of my brother, from the hand of Esau, for I am afraid of him; he may come and kill us all, the mothers with the children. Yet you have said, 'I will surely do you good, and make your offspring as the sand of the sea, which cannot be counted because of their number'" *(Genesis 32:11-12).*

Pray this prayer:

Dear God,

I come to you at this hour admitting that I need your deliverance. I am also offering up all of my concerns that are plaguing my mind. God you promised that you will always keep me in your arms. This is my prayer in Jesus name. Amen.

Action Plan

1. Make certain that you spend each day in prayer with God. Dates and times may be helpful.

2. For one month write out your prayers to God.

3. When praying, do not be general, be specific and allow room for God to answer however God chooses.

Chapter 6

God Is Pushing You to Your Destiny

Walk with your Limp

When you begin to have challenges in life sometimes it is not the Devil who's on your back.

God has a very interesting personality trait. The personality trait is that often times God will design specific situations that will cause you to be all alone where it will be just be you and God. This divinely orchestrated "kairos" moment (God's time) will sometimes occur when it is not at all convenient for you. This is exactly what happened to Jacob. *Jacob was left alone; and a man wrestled with him until daybreak* (Genesis 32:24).

There will come a time in your life when God will intentionally cause night to come into your life. I must admit, this concept is indeed foreign for many people and difficult to accept. I mean we as humans can get beside ourselves and become so busy with what I call busy work to the point that we forget who gives us the ability to even live.

Whenever God is trying to get your attention in order to push you to a destiny that He has designed specifically for you, it can be downright scary. Sadly, many people may not even be aware of the fact that God is possibly trying to get their attention. Therefore, God will purposely create a period in your life that I like to refer to as time-out.

Child of God, please know that God has a way of positioning you to a place where you will have to face God all by yourself. God will jump on your back if that is what is necessary in order for you to be still long enough for God to get you to chill out.

This is God's attitude with all of us from time to time. God says 'Okay, since you are so busy, and since you do not have enough sense to see that I am the One who gives you the power to accumulate wealth, I will place you in time-out for a season.' A season could be one day. A season could be one year, five years, or even longer. When God places you in time-out, it is in order to get your attention. The time-out will in essence be night in your life. No one enjoys having time-out in their life. Time-out can be a frightening and un-pleasurable time. I mean who really enjoys having to deal with challenges, frustrations, and difficulties when they are all alone!

Time-out is when you are in total isolation from the world. You are isolated from your family, friends, colleagues, and perhaps activities that you routinely enjoy. Please understand that it is quite possible that you very well may be in the presence of your family, friends, and colleagues, but you will still feel isolated, coupled with uneasiness on the inside of you. Sometimes it is the uneasiness that is doing somersaults on the inside of you that causes you to have a hunger and a desire for there to be more in your life. It is during this period of time-out in your isolation that God begins to conduct some of the most transformative work on you and in you that will eventually propel you to the next level in your life.

Jacob was now in a situation where absolutely no one could aid him. He was literally wrestling with divinity. This is already an uneven match. How in the world does a human defeat God by going toe-to-toe in a wrestling match?

During your time-out and isolation God is attempting to communicate to you that He has wonderful blessings for you. However, before God unveils the next step that He has for you there are some old ways that He will begin to transform in your life. You should be glad that God knows what's best for you. You should also be ecstatic that before God allows you to walk in the blessings that are in store for you, God will first clean you up in such a way that when the world sees the new you, they will not be able to believe it's you.

God will take you through a process where you are purged from old habits and desires. A part of the purging process could include the eradication of destructive habits and desires such as promiscuous living, jealously, greed, egotism, self-righteousness, hanging onto past hurts, and deceit. God is communicating to you that you are being purged in your time-out period of being estranged from God and you find yourself being drawn to God.

You may even notice that during your time-out period you begin to pray more than you have prayed before in your life. You may find yourself fasting, longing to be at church, and never wanting to leave the presence of God.

Unfortunately, people will often begin to fight against God during their time-out. You will find that people will even begin to put up the fight of their life, all in an effort to resist the destiny that God has carved out for them. Why the fight with God? I am inclined to believe that you fight against God because you are determined to have things your way and want to always be in total control. Fighting for many people also has to do with the fact that in spite of past indiscretions God has no interest in using them for His glory.

You should have figured out by now that God does not give a flying flip how sordid your past is. Perhaps gaining some insight on what happened to Jacob when he found himself alone will clarify things for you. You must understand that when you begin to have challenges in life, sometimes it is not the Devil who's on your back. It very well may be God body slamming you to the mat like a heavy weight wrestler. Please understand that when God has chosen you for a specific purpose in life there will be absolutely nothing you can do to escape it. Hence, it is not beneath God to hop on your back and begin to wrestle with you like you have never wrestled before. God can wrestle you to the point where God can cause you to have a limp. That's why it is imperative that you are always tuned in to the voice of God. If you are not tuned into the voice of God, God will literally do whatever God has to in order to get your attention.

Ask yourself how you are wrestling with God?   Perhaps you are fighting against God about going back to school to finish your degree. You have hit a glass ceiling at your job and God is telling you that you will not advance until you yield to what God is calling you to do. Perhaps you are fighting against God with decisions, sovereignty, finances, or relationship issues. Whatever you are wrestling with God about, I have news for you. You will not win until you yield to what God is doing in your life.

If God has to wrestle with you for one week, God will do it. If God has to wrestle with you for several years, God will do it. God will do whatever God has to do. Therefore, you might as well make today your last day of fighting against God and decide to get on the same page as God. Today would be an excellent time to ask God to please stop body slamming you. Today would be an excellent day for you to see and accept the blessings that God has for you.

In Genesis 32 this is exactly what is happening. God has apparently entered into an unsolicited wrestling match with Jacob. However, one thing you have to give Jacob credit for is that even though he realized that he was outmatched against his opponent who was God, all Jacob could do was hang onto God for dear life. That's a lesson we can all learn right there.

You must get to the point in your life where you develop the attitude that if God is going to put His hands on you, then you might as well hold onto God until God blesses you. Your blessing, breakthrough, deliverance, or miracle will not come until you learn to stop fighting with God and begin to yield to where and what God is positioning you for. The limp that you may incur from wrestling with God can serve as a reminder of the fact that you have had an encounter with God. Not only can your limp serve as a reminder of your wrestling match with God, but you should also know that there is absolutely no way that you can have an encounter with God and not leave changed for the rest of your life.

Jacob was left alone; and a man wrestled with him until daybreak. When the man saw that he did not prevail against Jacob, he struck him on the hip socket; and Jacob's hip was put out of joint as he wrestled with him. Then he said, "Let me go, for the day is breaking." But Jacob said, "I will not let you go, unless you bless me" (Genesis 32:24-26).

Jacob has been wrestling with God throughout the middle of the night. God says to Jacob "Let me go." Jacob says "I will not let you go unless you bless me." It is at this point that God touches Jacob in the hollow of his thigh and causes it to become disjointed. It is important for you to know that God did not put His full force behind touching Jacob on his hip. Yet, God actually touched his hip. This is an important point. This is important because perhaps Jacob did not realize that while God was body slamming him, God did not kill him. Throughout the wrestling match God kept Jacob in the palm of God's hand. This my friend is God demonstrating that while you may have to be body slammed, God will still shower you with grace. God displays His grace and mercy towards Jacob by not crushing Jacob to the point that it could have killed him. God touches Jacob just enough to cause him to incur a limp.

Just as God has kept Jacob under His grace, God does the same for you as well. Imagine, as you look back over your life at situations that God has brought you through. Have you ever wondered why you were never completely wiped out? When God begins to work on you, **God** will not stop until **God** brings forth the destiny that **God** desires. You can fight all you want to. You may have even been headed one way in life, but God decided to redirect you to another path.

God has a unique way of completely changing the direction you are headed in life and setting you on a course that is filled with blessings if you will only yield. God will ensure that your every need is provided for. What you must understand is that anytime God lays His hands on you, there may quite possibly be a severe impairment. Limps may be inflicted upon you that you should never be embarrassed about!

The limp that you may have in life should not be hidden. The limp is a symbol that, despite the challenge, it is to serve as a reminder for you that God's grace is sufficient for you. It may also serve to remind you that without God operating in your life, there is no way possible for you to accomplish the mission that

God has designed you for. Remember the next time you have to endure your limp, that God's grace is sufficient for you.

The limp that you may have in life is nothing to be embarrassed about. The limp should serve to remind you that because God is operating in your life you can do all things through Christ who strengthens you. The limp can signify that if it had not been for the Lord on your side, where would you be?

The limp reminds me of a story I heard once about an elderly lady whose granddaughter was ashamed of her grandmother's appearance whenever she would come to the local elementary school to pick her up. The grandmother had burns that were on her body that never quite healed properly. Every time the grandmother would come to pick up the little girl the other kids would begin to make comments under their breath. The grandmother may have had burns, she was not deaf. As the grandmother would pass by the other children in the hall way, they would begin to jeer and sneer at her. The children could be just downright mean with the cold callous comments they would make under their breath.

The little girl could not stand it. Finally, one day after the little girl had enough of receiving the butt of mean and terrible comments she asked her grandmother with tears streaming down her face. "Grandma, why do you have these scars all over your body? Grandma I know I shouldn't say this, but I am embarrassed when you come to my school because everyone picks at you and you never say anything back to them. Grandma, why do you do this?"

The little girl's grandma replied to her "Sweetie let me tell you why I don't have to say anything to the other kids at your school. You see the little kids don't know my story. When you were barely two years old my old home caught fire. The flames consumed the home within seconds. The firefighters said that they had done all they could to rescue everyone from the house, and that they did not see any more people in the house. I told the firefighters that you were in the house. They said that there was no way anyone could still be alive. Sweetie, grandmamma broke away from the firefighters and I ran back into the room I knew you would have been in to come and rescue you. You were sound asleep as scorching hot flames were all around you. Not one hair on your head was burned, but I received burns all over my body. You see sweetie, I chose to go into the fire to bring you out. So the burns that are all over my body are a symbol of how God was with me as I went through the fire to rescue you."

The little girl was moved to tears. The little girl could not help but give her grandmother a huge hug and apologize for her being embarrassed by the burn marks that were all over her grandmother's body. The little girl made a vow right there on the spot and told her grandmother that she would never be ashamed of the burn marks that she had. The little girl said that she felt honored that her grandmother thought enough of her to brave the scorching flames all in an effort to see to it that she was not consumed by the flames.

Your limp is nothing to be ashamed about. Who would have ever thought that Jesus Himself would show a limp that He incurred.

But Thomas (who was called the Twin), one of the twelve, was not with them when Jesus came. So the other disciples told him, "We have seen the Lord." But he said to them, "Unless I see the mark of the nails in his hands, and put my finger in the mark of the nails and my hand in his side, I will not believe."

A week later his disciples were again in the house, and Thomas was with them. Although the doors were shut, Jesus came and stood among them and said, "Peace be with you." Then he said to Thomas, "Put your finger here and see my hands. Reach out your hand and put it in my side. Do not doubt but believe." Thomas answered him, "My Lord and my God!" Jesus said to him, "Have you believed because you have seen me? Blessed are those who have not seen and yet have come to believe" (John 20:24-29).

The limp that you have is undoubtedly visible for the entire world to see. However, just because your limp is visible does not mean that God will not be with you. As we examine Jacob, we learn that, despite his limp, God continued to use him mightily. With a limp God continued to bless Jacob beyond his wildest dreams with wealth, family, and business acumen.

With your limp, you can still start that business. With your limp, you can still compete for promotions on your job. With your limp, you can grace a pulpit and preach sermons that are on fire from God. It is with your limp that as long as you keep moving, God will continue to bless. Your limp can be a perpetual reminder that even though you may have a handicap in the eyes of people, you can still do great and mighty things by Christ Jesus working in and through you.

You should view the limp from the lens that God is in the process of refining you to a perfect work. Humans may see you as imperfect. God sees you where a perfect work can be completed through you. There are many people even today who still refer to Jacob as trickster. These same people seem to forget that it was from the loins of Jacob that the twelve tribes came forth. It was also from the loins of Jacob that Jesus was born. Jesus' birth line came through the tribe of Judah. Recall that God took what was an imperfect situation in Jacob's eyes and allowed Judah to be born from Jacob's wife Leah, whom Jacob was not even crazy about. Understand that this does not mean that you are perfect. This means that God can take imperfect people and produce perfect work. In short, God can define your destiny through the limp that He has caused you.

While Jacob had a limp, Jacob did not allow himself to develop a victim mentality. Jacob did not understand how God was going to bring to past the vision that He had given him. Jacob only knew that God always kept His word. Therefore, Jacob only had the promise to operate from that God would accomplish what God said He would do; even with his limp.

The truth is we view a lot of people who have seemingly done outstanding things in life as super humans. Beethoven was one of the world's greatest classical pianists, yet he was deaf. That's a limp. Oprah Winfrey was told she was too fat to be on television, and America was not ready to see a Black person (especially a Black woman) in that light. That's a limp. Oprah Winfrey went on to have one of the greatest daytime television shows of all time and is also a billionaire. Harland Sanders, better known as Colonel Sanders of Kentucky Fried Chicken (KFC) did not start frying his signature fried chicken until he was forty years old. He had an age limp. In addition to this,

Colonel Sanders did not begin franchising KFC until he was sixty-five years old. That's a limp.

All of the above individuals endured severe limps in their lives. Nevertheless, they did not allow their limps to prevent them from accomplishing what God had created them for. We all have limps that we must bear in life. Perhaps your limp is a physical handicap. For another the limp may be their sex, race, age, finances or a dysfunctional family situation. Regardless, you must learn to persevere with your limp in spite of the challenges that it presents. Remember: *"You can do all things through Christ who strengthens you" (Philippians 4:13).*

What your limp also does for you is serve as a reminder that you must have God on your side to succeed. When God revealed Himself to Jacob through the dream, God told Jacob that He would always be with him: *"Know that I am with you and will keep you wherever you go, and will bring you back to this land; for I will not leave you until I have done what I have promised you" (Genesis 28:15).*

This is hallelujah shouting news! You have nothing to fear, nothing to be embarrassed about, and no reason to always explain yourself to others. God is with you, even with your limp.

No longer will you be defined by your past, you will be defined by your future. This will really upset people because they will see that you are no longer defined by your past, but God has chosen you. That's why you can operate at such a level that blows peoples' minds. The evidence of anointing is all over you, and they cannot stand to see how you are flowing and operating in your call.

When God is transforming you, your life and your call will not always look the way you would think it should look. You may not look the way you think you ought to look but you should thank God that God kept you.

There's too much in you to stay still. Do not hide your limp. People will and are talking about you, but nevertheless God has impregnated you with too much destiny to stay curled up in a corner. Your limp also serves as a testimony that others can be blessed by hearing and/or seeing. More importantly, your limp signifies that you are totally dependent on God to see you through. There was a time in your life where you operated under your own devices, but now that you are walking in your call you need God every hour. Just as the song says *"I Need Thee Every Hour."* You must always remember to keep your hand in God's hand, even with your limp.

➢ Blessings Go Two Ways

We can bless the Lord with how we live our lives on a day to day basis. To bless the Lord is not just what you say, but you also bless the Lord by how you live. Many people choose not to bless the Lord because they are under the allusion that it was their own wit, their own intellect or finances that brought them to where they are in their life. What is even more amazing is how these same people will pray so fervently for the Lord to bless them. These same people will pray prayers for God to open doors and provide opportunities, yet when God grants them the desires of their hearts they forget who answered their prayers.

In other words, they now suffer from amnesia. As a result of their amnesia they become totally oblivious to the fact that had it not been for the Lord on their side, where would they be? Also, God warns us that it would be in our best interest to bless Him. The scripture below suggests that you remember it was God who has brought you out of wilderness situations. Perhaps your wilderness situation was a bad relationship. Maybe your wilderness situation was unpaid bills, or even a health situation. For some their wilderness situation was that they knew they were no good for heaven, but unfit to die so they just needed God to come into their life to do a major job on them. Regardless of the situation or situations, God desires for everyone to remember that it was He who brought you through. Take a moment to examine the scripture below:

> *The clothes on your back did not wear out and your feet did not swell these forty years. Know then in your heart that as a parent disciplines a child so the LORD your God disciplines you. Therefore, keep the commandments of the LORD your God, by walking in his ways and by fearing him. For the LORD your God is bringing you into a good land, a land with flowing streams, with springs and underground waters welling up in valleys and hills, a land of wheat and barley, of vines and fig trees and pomegranates, a land of olive trees and honey, a land where you may eat bread without scarcity, where you will lack nothing, a land whose stones are iron and from whose hills you may mine copper. You shall eat your fill and bless the LORD your God for the good*

land that he has given you. Take care that you do not forget the LORD your God, by failing to keep his commandments, his ordinances, and his statutes, which I am commanding you today. When you have eaten your fill and have built fine houses and live in them, and when your herds and flocks have multiplied, and your silver and gold is multiplied, and all that you have is multiplied, then do not exalt yourself, forgetting the LORD your God, who brought you out of the land of Egypt, out of the house of slavery, who led you through the great and terrible wilderness, an arid wasteland with poisonous snakes and scorpions. He made water flow for you from flint rock, and fed you in the wilderness with manna that your ancestors did not know, to humble you and to test you, and in the end to do you good. Do not say to yourself, "My power and the might of my own hand have gotten me this wealth." But remember the LORD your God, for it is he who gives you power to get wealth, so that he may confirm his covenant that he swore to your ancestors, as he is doing today. If you do forget the LORD your God and follow other gods to serve and worship them, I

solemnly warn you today that you shall
surely perish (Deuteronomy 8:4-20).

Jacob clearly understood the importance of blessing the Lord. Genesis 28:10-17 shows that once Jacob became aware of the many blessings that God had in store for him he could not help but become overjoyed.

More interesting is that Jacob made a vow right where he was that from that moment on he would always give to God at least one-tenth of all that God would bless him with. I would like to suggest that this is why many people never walk in all that God has for them. They are unwilling to give back to God (bless God) a portion of what God has already blessed them with.

It is as if many people view the blessings of God as a one-way street. Consider that a lot of people have no problem praying to God that God bless their finances, or bless their marriage, or to bless this or bless that. Well, guess what! God desires that you bless Him as well. In fact, God even challenges people to bless him and see if He will not begin to bless you beyond your wildest dreams.

A sad truth is that one of the reasons you may not be receiving all that God has for you is simply because you refuse to bless God back. I love what the prophet Malachi says:

You are cursed with a curse, for you are
robbing me—the whole nation of you!
Bring the full tithe into the storehouse,
so that there may be food in my house,
and thus put me to the test, says the
LORD of hosts; see if I will not open the
windows of heaven for you and pour

down for you an overflowing blessing
(Malachi 3:9-10).

This is as clear as it gets. Blessings are not a one-way street with regards to your relationship with God. Jacob understood this well. As you examine the life of Jacob, we can clearly see that even though Jacob had a questionable pass, he had no question of who sustained him, who kept him, and who protected him. Therefore, Jacob had no problem blessing God.

Child of God, turn this book down for a few seconds, pause, and begin to bless God right where you are. Bless God for not allowing you to lose your sanity when you were in insane situations. Bless God for blessing you with the ability to earn an income. Bless God for blessing you with enough of a mind to not be illiterate and to be able to read this book. Determine that from this day forward you will never be ungrateful or take for granted the blessings that God has bestowed upon you. Lastly, give God praise that God chose to bless you to be a blessing to others.

Think About It

1. Can you recall a period in your life when you noticed that things were in disarray only to later realize that God was repositioning you on a course that God would have you to be on?

_____

_____

_____

2. Has God ever placed you in a night season in life? If so, how did you handle it? How long did your night last, or are you in a night situation now?

_____

_____

_____

3. Consider a challenging situation you have been in and contemplate how God's grace was with you?

_____

_____

_____

4. Why do you feel that God uses imperfect people (with limps) to engage in perfect work?

_____

_____

_____

5. Have you ever had a moment in life where you felt so honored that God favored you to the point you could not wait to bless God back?

_____

_____

_____

6. Why do you think Jacob had no problem blessing God?

_____

_____

_____

Reflect On It

"But remember the LORD your God, for it is he who gives you power to get wealth, so that he may confirm his covenant that he swore to your ancestors, as he is doing today. If you do forget the LORD your God and follow other gods to serve and worship them, I solemnly warn you today that you shall surely perish" (Deuteronomy8:18-20).

When the man saw that he did not prevail against Jacob, he struck him on the hip socket; and Jacob's hip was put out of joint as he wrestled with him. Then he said, "Let me go, for the day is breaking." But Jacob said, "I will not let you go, unless you bless me" (Genesis32:26).

Pray this prayer:

Dear God,

I will not let you go under any circumstances. Even with my limp, I still need you in my life. I cannot make it without you. Thank You for all you have done for me. Thank you for the manifold blessings that you have equipped me with. Thank you for not just blessing me, but for blessing me to be a blessing to others, In Jesus name I pray. Amen.

Action Plan

1. This week take time out of your schedule and intentionally bless someone with the gifts God has blessed you with.

2. Starting when you rise early in the morning before your feet hit the floor tell God thank you for the manifold blessings that God has equipped you with.

3. Determine that this will be the last day that you hide the limp that you have in your life. Your days of embarrassment are over.

4. Resolve today that all you have from God is God's promise. God has been faithful to you, therefore begin

to walk in your destiny with your limp and trust God that a way will be made.

5. Make up your mind that today is the last day you will use your limp as an excuse for not moving into action.

Epilogue

Get Moving

Exercise Your Faith

You will never be able to walk in the blessings God has for you until you learn to walk by faith, and not by sight.

You must develop a mentality and a mindset that you can do all things through Christ Who strengthens you. You must declare out loud every time you begin to feel inadequate and unqualified that God's grace is sufficient for you. Child of God, I firmly believe that just as the Bible says: "You have been trustworthy in a few things; I will put you in charge of many things" (*Matthew 25:23*). You will never be able to walk in the blessings God has for you until you learn to: *"Walk by faith, and not by sight"* (2nd Corinthians 5:7).

What we have to do in order to continue to pursue and to receive the blessings of God is to show God that we can be faithful over the little things that we have right now. One of the main reasons that you may not be walking in the overflow is because you are still trying to figure everything out by yourself, as opposed to hanging onto God and allowing God to lead and guide you.

So what if you may not have a business yet. Have you exercised your faith by writing out your business plan? So what if you may not have been accepted to a college yet? Have you exercised your faith by filling out entrance applications? So what if you are not married yet? Do you exercise your faith by keeping up your appearance and refrain from participating in gossip to make yourself attractable to a suitable mate? Maybe you desire for God to bless you with a new home. Have you exercised your faith by beginning to repair the damaged credit you may have and curtail your bad spending habits by saving money for the down payment?

Why do people feel that God will continue to roll blessings out when they have not demonstrated that they will walk by faith with what they have already been blessed with? Please don't get it wrong, and don't get it twisted! In no way am I implying that just because you do "A", "B" will automatically happen. All I'm attempting to relay is that you must be faithful over the little you do have, and then God will continue to pour out more and more blessings in your life.

Please recall the parable of the talents. Because two of the stewards demonstrated their faith by working with what they did have, the Lord not only grew what they had, but the Lord also honored them for operating in faith. However, there was one steward who buried what he was blessed with. Because he buried the talent that he was blessed with, the talent never multiplied and the Lord took from him his talent and blessed someone else with the talent.

Child of God, you must work with what God has already blessed you with. As you demonstrate your faithfulness, commitment, and determination, God will honor the effort that you are making. You must demonstrate that you will not allow your handicaps and or what you don't have to be used as a license for you to give up and not go after what God has birthed in you.

About the Author

Carlton Worthen is a "Florida Boy," and is the oldest child of Rev. & Mrs. Charlie C. Worthen. Carlton was born and raised in the Capital City of Tallahassee, Florida, and attended the prestigious Florida A&M University (FAMU). Carlton received his Bachelor of Science Degree in Political Science, with a minor in Public Administration. Carlton has his Master of Divinity Degree (M.Div.) from Turner Theological Seminary of The Interdenominational Theological Center (ITC), with a concentration in Homiletics and Worship, and was commended for receiving one of the highest honors in his class.

Carlton was known as one of Tallahassee's favorite talk show hosts, as the host of "*C.W. Presents.*" He brought fresh perspectives that were both engaging and entertaining to his audience. In 2004, Carlton produced and hosted a city wide symposium in Tallahassee, Florida, *"Make Your Vote Count."* The symposium was targeted to individuals encouraging them to turn out and vote during the 2004 presidential elections between President George W. Bush and Senator John Kerry.

Carlton's many accomplishments have included being a top adviser to former Mayor/Commissioner of Tallahassee, Dorothy Inman-Johnson, providing volunteer and consulting services to U.S. Representative Allan Boyd, D-Florida, Leon County Commissioner Cliff Thaell and to former candidate for the Leon County Commission, Bob Henderson. Worthen has also served on the Board of Directors for the 2-1-1 Big Bend, a subsidiary of The United Way.

Carlton has always had a love for God and a passion for God's word. Carlton accepted his calling in 2005, and thus strives to fulfill God's calling on his life. In 2007, Carlton was selected to participate in ITC's distinguished program "Faith

Journey", a program which selects only the "chosen few" students who demonstrate superb academic excellence and extraordinary promise in parish ministry.

In 2008, God encouraged Carlton to begin "The Empowerment Ministries" in Atlanta, Georgia, and charged Carlton to plant this ministry into the lives of others. "The Empowerment Ministries" is a ministry that seeks to foster uninhibited and dynamic praise and worship, social and political activism, and dedicated service to the community, empowerment to pastors and congregations, and financial growth.

In 2011, Carlton was elected by the Turner Theological Seminary Alumni/ae to serve as their national President.

In 2012, Carlton provided the keynote address to the Barnesville, Georgia Lamar county NAACP Annual Banquet.

Currently, Carlton is the Senior Pastor of St. John A.M.E. Church in Eufaula, Alabama.

Carlton lives by the motto, *"Be prosperous in all that you do."* Carlton spends his spare time watching comedy movies, reading, resting on the sandy beaches of Florida and attending FAMU football games.

www.ingramcontent.com/pod-product-compliance
Lightning Source LLC
LaVergne TN
LVHW051151080426
835508LV00021B/2580